X

# EXPLORERS!

# Lewis and Clark

## American Explorers

*Arlene Bourgeois Molzahn*

 **Enslow Publishers, Inc.**

| 40 Industrial Road | PO Box 38 |
|---|---|
| Box 398 | Aldershot |
| Berkeley Heights, NJ 07922 | Hants GU12 6BP |
| USA | UK |

http://www.enslow.com

To my granddaughter Maria, for all the wonderful times we have shared.

**Library of Congress Cataloging-in-Publication Data**

Molzahn, Arlene Bourgeois.
    Lewis and Clark : American explorers / Arlene Bourgeois Molzahn.
        p. cm. — (Explorers!)
    Summary: Discusses Lewis and Clark's journey of discovery to the Pacific Ocean.
    Includes bibliographical references and index.
    ISBN 0-7660-2067-3
        1. Lewis and Clark Expedition (1804–1806)—Juvenile literature. 2. West (U.S.)—
Discovery and exploration—Juvenile literature. [1. Lewis and Clark Expedition (1804–1806)
2. Lewis, Meriwether, 1774–1809. 3. Clark, William, 1770-1838. 4. Explorers. 5. West (U.S.)—
Discovery and exploration.]  I. Title. II. Explorers! (Enslow Publishers)
F592.7 .M645 2003
917.804'2'0922—dc21                                        2002005115

Printed in the United States of America

10 9 8 7 6 5 4 3 2 1

**To Our Readers:** We have done our best to make sure all Internet Addresses in this book were active and appropriate when we went to press. However, the author and the publisher have no control over and assume no liability for the material available on those Internet sites or on other Web sites they may link to. Any comments or suggestions can be sent by e-mail to comments@enslow.com or to the address on the back cover.

Every effort has been made to locate all copyright holders of material used in this book. If any errors or omissions have occurred, corrections will be made in future editions of this book.

**Illustration credits:** © 1999 Artville, LLC., p. 7, 22; Corel Corporation, pp. 27, 28, 36, 39, 40; Dover Publications, Inc., p. 4 (inset); Judith Edwards, pp. 1, 18, 19, 21, 24, 34, 42; Enslow Publishers, Inc., p. 6, 41; Library of Congress, pp. 4, 8, 10, 11, 12, 13, 14, 16, 20, 22 (inset), 25, 26, 30, 31, 32, 33, 38.

**Cover Illustration:** background, Monster Zero Media; photo of statue, Judith Edwards.

Please note: Compasses on the cover and in the book are from © 1999 Artville, LLC.

Statue photo: This statue is in Great Falls, Montana. Lewis and Clark are standing; York is kneeling with Lewis's dog Seaman.

# Contents

List of Maps

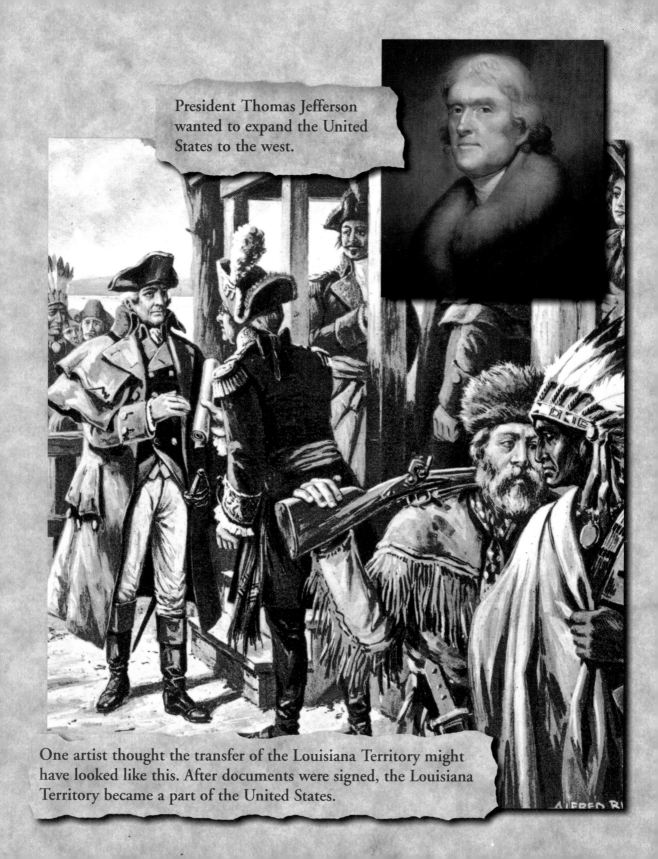

President Thomas Jefferson wanted to expand the United States to the west.

One artist thought the transfer of the Louisiana Territory might have looked like this. After documents were signed, the Louisiana Territory became a part of the United States.

# Before the Great Adventure

In 1801, the United States was made up of land from the Atlantic Ocean to the Mississippi River. President Thomas Jefferson hoped that one day the United States would reach from the Atlantic Ocean to the Pacific Ocean.

The French owned the Louisiana Territory, a large area of land west of the Mississippi River. Jefferson sent men to Paris, France, where they offered almost $10 million to buy New Orleans. The French offered to sell all of Louisiana to the United States for $15 million.

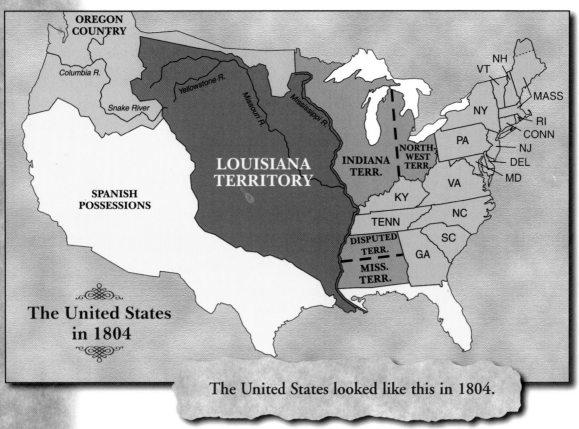

The United States looked like this in 1804.

On April 30, 1803, the United States agreed. This became known as the Louisiana Purchase.

At this time maps of this land were not correct. So, President Jefferson searched for the right man to explore the new territory. This man needed to be able to make friends with the American Indian tribes that lived on this land. He had to be able to write down information about

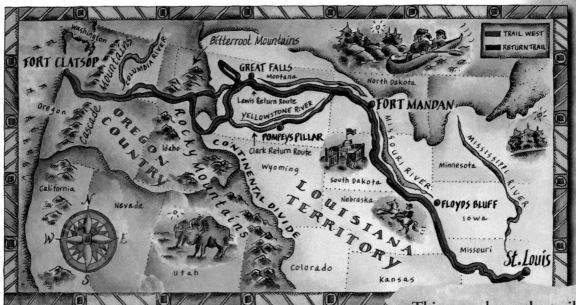

This map shows the trail traveled by the Corps of Discovery.

the plants and animals of the area. He would also have to be able to make maps and be a good leader.

President Jefferson asked Meriwether Lewis to lead the expedition. Lewis agreed to do so only if William Clark could go, too. Clark was made cocaptain of the expedition. After Clark said yes, they began to get ready for the trip.

William Clark

Meriwether Lewis

# Early Years of the Explorers

## William Clark

William Clark was born on August 1, 1770, in Caroline County, Virginia. Clark was the ninth of ten children. His father had a large farm. When Clark was fifteen years old, the family moved to Kentucky. At that time, Kentucky was a wilderness with no towns and no schools.

Clark did not have much schooling, but he knew a lot about farming. He knew all about the plants that grew in the area. He understood the ways of the wild animals that roamed the woods near his home.

William Clark grew up in Kentucky. It was a wilderness in the 1700s.

William Clark joined the Kentucky Militia when he was nineteen years old. He later joined the United States Army. There was trouble between the American Indians and the settlers in Ohio. Clark and the army were there to keep the peace.

Clark liked the army life. He was a sharpshooter in the Chosen Rifle Company. Soon, he was made captain. He met Meriwether Lewis and found him to be honest and trusting. Clark learned a lot about the different American

Indian tribes. He respected their ways of life. Clark also had a great love for the wilderness.

In 1796, the trouble in Ohio ended. Clark left the army. He wanted a life of adventure. He had planned to travel on the Mississippi River. He hoped to make a living trading with the American Indians living along the river. But because of problems at home in Kentucky, he had to give up that idea.

William Clark respected the American Indians and their way of life.

## Meriwether Lewis

Meriwether Lewis was born in Albemarle County, Virginia, on August 18, 1774. He was the second of three children. His father died when he was five years old. His mother was left alone to run the family plantation with three young children. She soon remarried.

There were schools in those days, but not like the ones we have today. So Lewis was taught at home until he was thirteen years old. Then, from the age of thirteen to eighteen, he went to school. He learned grammar, math,

This is how a farm looked in the 1700s.

Lewis and Clark did not have schools like the ones we have today. Their classroom might have looked like this.

science, and Latin. Living on a large plantation, Lewis learned to be a good horseman. He also learned to be a good hunter and hiker. When Lewis was eighteen years old, his stepfather died. Lewis had to take over running the plantation.

As a young man, Meriwether Lewis heard about a need for soldiers. In 1794, he joined the army. He loved camping in tents under the stars at night. He liked seeing

Lewis posed for this painting in 1807.

different parts of the country. Lewis decided to stay in the army, even after it was no longer needed on the frontier.

While in the army, Lewis traveled up and down the Ohio River on a large flat-bottom boat called a keelboat. He was an army paymaster. He visited different forts along the river. Later he became a member of the Chosen Rifle Company. This was a group of men who were very good at shooting rifles. The captain of the company was William Clark.

By 1800, Lewis had become a captain in the army. In 1801, Captain Lewis became the personal secretary to President Thomas Jefferson.

William Clark and Meriwether Lewis were to become two very important explorers.

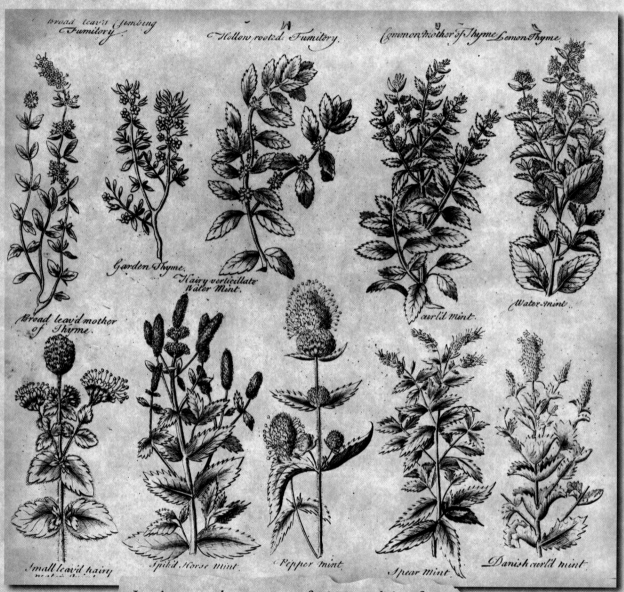

Broad leav'd Climbing Fumitory.

Hollow rooted Fumitory.

Common Mother of Thyme Lemon Thyme.

Garden Thyme.

Hairy verticillate Water Mint.

Water-mint.

curl'd mint.

Broad leav'd mother of Thyme.

Small leav'd hairy

Spiked Horse Mint.

Pepper mint.

Spear Mint.

Danish curl'd mint.

Lewis spent the summer of 1803 studying for the journey. He learned about different types of herbs. Herbs could be used for medicines and for cooking.

# Planning and Preparing

Lewis and Clark had to find about thirty other men who knew something about the wilderness. They had to be men who could be trusted and were willing to be away from home for a very long time. This group called themselves the Corps of Discovery.

Meriwether Lewis spent the summer of 1803 studying. He had to learn about the stars, plants, animals, and medicine. He had to learn how to take correct measurements and how to make maps.

Supplies for the long trip had to be bought. Special instruments like compasses, telescopes, and

York, shown here on the far left, traveled with Lewis and Clark. This statue is in Great Falls, Montana.

## York

York was William Clark's slave companion, or manservant. Clark and York grew up together and were about the same age. York joined the Corps of Discovery where he helped to hunt, explore, and take care of people who were sick. York became the first African-American man to cross the country.

thermometers were needed. Other equipment such as pliers, handsaws, hatchets, fishing hooks, fishing lines, and mosquito curtains were bought. The men took along 12 pounds of soap, 3 bushels of salt, and 193 pounds of "portable soup." Portable soup was beef, eggs, and vegetables made into a paste. Water was added to the paste to make soup.

Warm clothing was needed. Blankets, woolen pants, shoes, flannel shirts, coats, stockings, and knapsacks were packed for the men. There would be no doctors along the way, so a good supply of medicine had to be taken along.

Guns were needed to shoot animals for food. They were also needed to protect the men from anyone or anything dangerous they might meet along the way. They collected 15 rifles, 420 pounds of lead for bullets, and 176 pounds of gunpowder for the trip. Different types of knives were taken, as well as many books about plants, stars, minerals, and navigation.

The men needed supplies, like these guns.

The men used keelboats to go up the Missouri River.

They took a large supply of gifts for the American Indians. Among the things they packed were 144 pocket mirrors, 4,600 sewing needles, 144 small scissors, and 10 pounds of thread. They also took silk ribbons, combs, yards of bright-colored cloth, 288 knives, 8 brass kettles, and 33 pounds of tiny colored beads.

Lewis drew up plans for a boat that could be taken apart if needed. This made it possible for the boat to be carried over land. This type of boat was called a keelboat. When the keelboat was put together, it could not hold all the men and supplies. Two smaller canoe-shaped boats were bought. A group of French boatmen were hired to handle the smaller boats.

Dugout canoes, like this one, were used by the explorers.

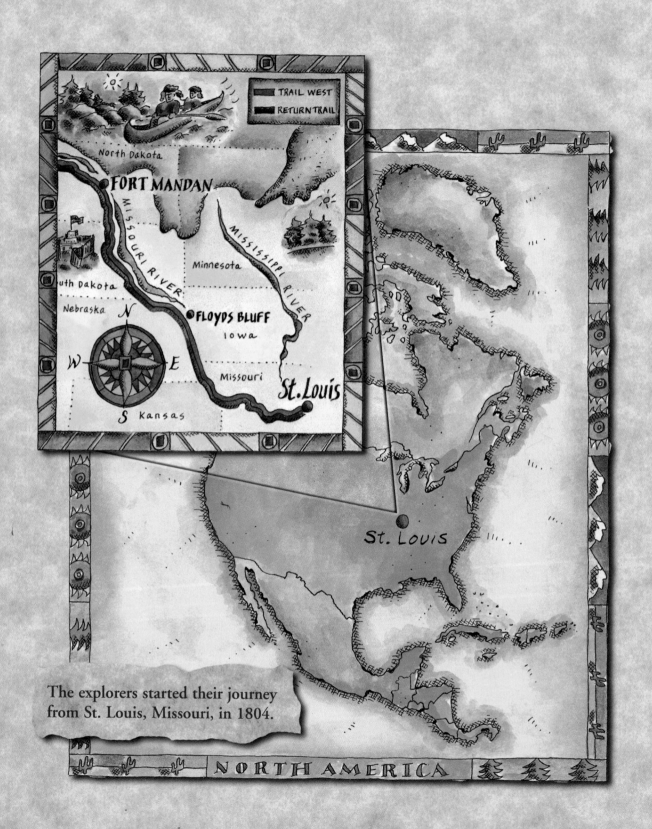

TRAIL WEST
RETURN TRAIL

North Dakota

**FORT MANDAN**

MISSOURI RIVER

MISSISSIPPI RIVER

Minnesota

uth Dakota

Nebraska

N

W    E

S    Kansas

**FLOYDS BLUFF**

Iowa

Missouri

**St. Louis**

St. Louis

The explorers started their journey
from St. Louis, Missouri, in 1804.

NORTH AMERICA

# The Voyage of Discovery

On May 14, 1804, the people of St. Louis, Missouri, gathered on the riverbank. They watched as one of the most important expeditions in American history began. Three boats loaded with men and supplies were beginning a great adventure up the Missouri River.

The Missouri River was a swift and dangerous river. The men used oars to row the boats up the river during the daytime. Sometimes they had to push long poles into the bottom of the river to move the boats ahead. On days when the wind blew from the right direction, the

### Seaman

Lewis bought a big Newfoundland dog before the trip and named the dog Seaman. Seaman went with the expedition. He rode in the boat with Lewis, but he sometimes swam to shore. Seaman ran back and forth chasing squirrels. When he caught a squirrel, he would bring it to Lewis. Seaman was a good friend to Lewis and went with him exploring.

Lewis's dog Seaman went with the Corps.

men raised sails on the boats. The boats moved very slowly on the river. They went about fifteen miles a day.

The men who were good hunters did not ride on the boats. They walked along the riverbank or took turns riding the two horses that had been brought along. They hunted deer, ducks, rabbits, geese, and other animals.

At night, everyone went ashore. They built campfires to keep warm, to dry out any wet clothing, and to cook a meal. They also made food for the next day because they did not stop to cook during the day. On days the hunters had been lucky, the men had fresh meat to eat. On other days, they ate dried food from the supplies they had brought along.

During the evening, some men fixed things that were wrong with the boats. They fixed broken poles and oars. At night, men guarded the camp from wild animals. They also watched for anyone who might steal their boats and supplies. After all the work was done, some

Some of the men hunted as they walked along the riverbank.

men played their fiddles, others sang, and some even danced. In bad weather, the men slept in small tents. In good weather, they slept under the stars.

Lewis walked along the shore most of the time. He collected plants and kept notes on the animals he saw along the way. Clark stayed on the keelboat. He took notes on the turns of the Missouri River to make his maps.

As the expedition moved upstream, mosquitoes and ticks made the men very uncomfortable. They had to

Sometimes the men ran into trouble on the river. At night, the men repaired their boats.

The explorers saw many different animals, such as antelope.

cover themselves with grease or stand in the smoke of their campfires to drive them away.

In the beginning of August 1804, everyone became worried about Sergeant Charles Floyd. He had been feeling sick for several days. By the middle of August, no one knew what to do to help him. Floyd died on August 20, 1804. He was buried on a hill overlooking the Missouri River near what is now Sioux City, Iowa. Sergeant Floyd was the first United States soldier to die west of the Mississippi River.

Many American Indian tribes lived in the lands that Lewis and Clark were exploring. This painting, by Charles M. Russell, shows American Indians discovering Lewis and Clark.

# New Lands, New People

As the explorers journeyed up the Missouri River, they saw plains of prairie grasses that were eight feet high. The explorers had their first meeting with American Indians on August 3, 1804. A small group of friendly American Indians from the Oto and Missouri tribes met with Lewis and Clark. An interpreter, who spoke both the languages of the tribes and English, helped them communicate. An interpreter is someone who listens to a person speak in one language and then tells what that person said in another language.

A few days later, eighteen year old George Shannon did not return from a day of hunting. Some men went to look for Shannon, who was the youngest man on the expedition. After several days, the expedition had to move on without him.

On August 30, 1804, the expedition had reached the territory where the Sioux lived. The Sioux were great hunters and brave fighters. Lewis and Clark met with the chiefs. Pierre Dorion, a Frenchman, spoke both English

The Sioux tribe helped Lewis and Clark. Sioux chiefs and the explorers exchanged gifts.

The meeting with the Sioux was a friendly one, and the expedition continued west.

and the Sioux language. He helped the chiefs and explorers understand each other. They smoked a peace pipe and exchanged gifts. This friendly meeting meant that the expedition could go on in peace.

One day near the end of September, shouts of joy went up from the boats. The men saw Shannon walking along the riverbank. He had followed the river hoping he would meet up with the expedition. Everyone was very happy to see Shannon again.

By October 25, 1804, the expedition had reached what today is the city of Bismarck, North Dakota. The Mandan and Hidatsa tribes lived in this area. Lewis and

Clark spent the next month building a fort there. They called it Fort Mandan. This is where they spent the first winter.

On November 4, 1804, a French trader named Toussaint Charbonneau and his wife Sacagawea joined the expedition. During that winter, a baby boy was born to Sacagawea and her husband. They named him Jean Baptiste. He was nicknamed Pomp, and traveled with the expedition.

On April 7, 1805, the expedition left Fort Mandan and once again began moving up the Missouri River. By

Lewis and Clark knew that to survive the winter they would need a well-built fort.

## Sacagawea

Sacagawea was a member of the Shoshone tribe. Sacagawea's name means Bird Woman. She was born in the Rocky Mountains area in about 1787 and lived with the Shoshone until she was about twelve years old. One day, a raiding party from the Hidatsa tribe came and stole horses from the Shoshone. They captured Sacagawea and brought her to their homes on the upper Missouri River. When she was about seventeen years old, Sacagawea was bought by a Frenchman named Toussaint Charbonneau. Sacagawea became his wife.

This is the Sacagawea Monument in Oregon.

Sacagawea could speak two American Indian languages. She helped Lewis and Clark by being an interpreter.

July 18, the expedition passed through the Gates of the Rocky Mountains. On August 8, Sacagawea saw a mountain called Beaver's Head. She told Lewis and Clark that the Shoshone lived just beyond the mountain.

Lewis set out to find the Shoshone villages. The expedition would need horses to cross the mountains

The Gates of the Rockies look like this today.

before winter. Lewis hoped to buy horses from the Shoshone. On August 17, Lewis, Clark, and Sacagawea met with Chief Cameahwait. Sacagawea began to tell Lewis and Clark what the chief was saying. Then suddenly, she stopped, jumped up, and put her arms around the chief. She knew him. He was her brother.

The Shoshone agreed to sell twenty-nine horses to the explorers because of Sacagawea. They also gave valuable information about the dangers and rough times ahead on the trail.

After leaving the Shoshone, the explorers traveled

over the Rocky Mountains and reached the Columbia River. The river had many rapids and narrow passages between huge rocks. The men feared for their lives many times. On November 17, 1805, the explorers reached the Pacific Ocean.

The explorers quickly set to work building a fort for the second winter of the expedition. They called their winter home Fort Clatsop in honor of the friendly Clatsop people who lived in the area. The expedition stayed at Fort Clatsop until March 23, 1806.

Then they began the long trip back to St. Louis, Missouri. To explore even more of the Louisiana Territory, Lewis and Clark split the group in two for the trip home. Lewis led one group through the mountains. Clark and the other group explored the Yellowstone River. In August, the two groups met at the Missouri River and headed to St. Louis together. On September 23, 1806, the explorers were very happy as they reached the end of their journey.

Many settlers headed west following the trail that Lewis and Clark had taken.

# The New Frontier

The Louisiana Territory was more than 800,000 square miles. It covered all or parts of what were to become thirteen western states. The cost of the land was three cents an acre. The Louisiana Purchase doubled the land size of the United States in 1803.

The Lewis and Clark Expedition is also called the Journey of Discovery. The expedition lasted two years and four months from May 14, 1804, to September 23, 1806.

The explorers returned from their journey with the first correct maps of the Missouri River. Their journey

The Corps of Discovery explored and mapped many areas, such as the Three Forks at the beginning of the Missouri River.

showed that there was no all-water route from the Missouri River to the Pacific Ocean. They also returned with the first maps of a section of the Rocky Mountains and the Columbia River. The explorers did find a land route that crossed over the Rocky Mountains to the Pacific Ocean.

Lewis and Clark found twenty-four American Indian tribes. They brought back information on the customs and languages of the tribes. They found 178 plants and 122 animals that were unknown in the eastern part of the

United States. Animals like pronghorn antelope, bull snakes, terns, prairie dogs, jackrabbits, grouse, and pelicans were all new to the explorers. Some of the explorers saw buffalo for the first time.

The expedition opened up the frontier for hunters and trappers. Soon settlers in covered wagons moved westward. They followed the route that Lewis and Clark had taken to the West. Many families settled in the

Lewis and Clark found many new plants and animals on their journey.

Oregon Country. The settlers helped make the Oregon Country part of the United States.

The expedition changed the lives of the American Indians forever. The settlers brought diseases with them as they settled the West. The medicine men of the tribes did not know how to treat these diseases. Sometimes whole tribes died from measles or smallpox.

The United States Congress gave all the explorers double pay at the end of the journey. They were also given the rights to 320 acres of land west of the

Thanks to Lewis and Clark, many people moved to the Oregon Country.

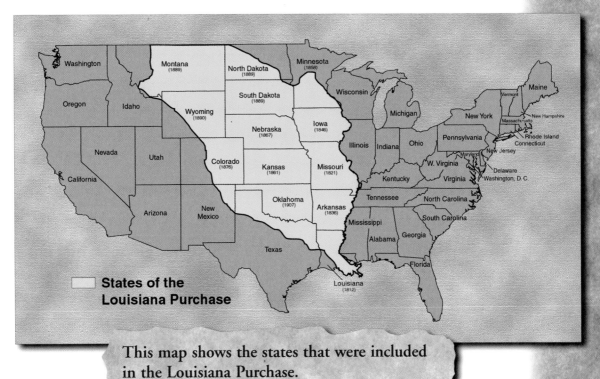

**States of the Louisiana Purchase**

This map shows the states that were included in the Louisiana Purchase.

Mississippi River. Many of the explorers settled on that land. Several of the men joined the army. Some went back to the mountains and became hunters and trappers. George Shannon became a lawyer and later a state senator for the state of Missouri.

Clark had promised Sacagawea that he would make sure her children had a good education. A few years after the expedition, Sacagawea and Charbonneau brought their two children, Jean Baptiste and Lizette, to St. Louis, Missouri. Clark kept his promise to Sacagawea, and he took over the education of her children.

No one is sure what happened to Sacagawea. Most people believe she died December 20, 1812. Others believe she died much later, in 1884.

Congress rewarded Lewis and Clark for a job well done by giving them each 1,600 acres of land. Clark

Today, people act out the adventures of Lewis and Clark. These people are performing what might have happened when Lewis and Clark met Sacagawea.

married and had five children. He was the Superintendent of Indian Affairs for Upper Louisiana. He later became the first governor of the Missouri Territory. He died at the age of sixty-eight and was buried in St. Louis, Missouri.

Lewis did not live long after the expedition ended. In 1807, he became governor of the Upper Louisiana Territory. But he missed the excitement of the wilderness. In 1809, Lewis died on his way to Washington, D.C.

Lewis and Clark will always be remembered for having been important explorers in one of America's great adventures.

# Timeline

**August 1, 1770**—William Clark was born in Caroline County, Virginia.

**August 18, 1774**—Meriwether Lewis was born in Albemarle County, Virginia.

**Fall 1802**—President Jefferson asks Lewis to lead an expedition.

**April 30, 1803**—The United States buys the Louisiana Territory; this is known as the Louisiana Purchase.

**May 14, 1804**—The expedition begins.

**November 4, 1804**—Sacagawea joins the expedition.

**November 17, 1805**—The Corps of Discovery reaches the Pacific Ocean.

**March 23, 1806**—The Corps leaves Fort Clatsop and starts for home.

**September 23, 1806**—The Corps of Discovery returns to St. Louis, Missouri.

# Words to Know

**corps**—A group of people working together for the same reason.

**expedition**—A journey or voyage taken for a special reason.

**explore**—To travel in little-known lands or seas.

**interpreter**—A person who explains another language or the meaning of something.

**keelboat**—A large boat that is not very deep and is used for hauling goods.

**paymaster**—A person whose job it is to pay wages to workers.

**plantation**—A very large farm usually found in the southern part of the United States.

**reward**—Something given to a person for a job well done.

**route**—A way to go, a road to take.

**secretary**—A person who writes letters and keeps records for another person or company.

**territory**—A land, an area, or a region.

# Learn More About
# Lewis and Clark

## Books

Bowen, Andy R. *Back of Beyond: A Story of Lewis and Clark*. Minneapolis, Minn.: Lerner, 1998.

Gunderson, Mary. *Cooking on the Lewis and Clark Expedition*. Minnetonka, Minn.: Capstone Press, Inc., 2000.

Morley, Jacqueline. *Across America: The Story of Lewis and Clark*. Danbury, Conn.: Franklin Watts, 1999.

Patent, Dorothy Hinshaw. *Animals on the Trail with Lewis and Clark*. New York, N.Y.: Houghton Mifflin Company, 2002.

Roop, Peter and Connie Roop. *Off the Map: The Journals of Lewis and Clark*. New York: Walker & Co., 1998.

Schanzer, Rosalyn. *How We Crossed the West: The Adventures of Lewis and Clark*. Washington, D.C.: National Geographic Society, 2002.

St. George, Judith. *Sacagawea*. New York: G. P. Putnam, 1997.

# Learn More About
# Lewis and Clark

## Internet Addresses

### The Journey of the Corps of the Discovery

<www.pbs.org/lewisandclark/>

*This site has a lot of information about Lewis and Clark.*

### Lewis and Clark: On the Trail

<http://lewisandclark.state.mt.us/discovery.shtm>

*Find out more neat facts about Lewis and Clark from the state of Montana.*

# Index